Incarnation

Incarnation

Daily Poems for Advent

SKYA ABBATE

RESOURCE *Publications* • Eugene, Oregon

INCARNATION
Daily Poems for Advent

Copyright © 2013 Skya Abbate. All rights reserved. Except for brief quotations in critical publications or reviews, no part of this book may be reproduced in any manner without prior written permission from the publisher. Write: Permissions, Wipf and Stock Publishers, 199 W. 8th Ave., Suite 3, Eugene, OR 97401.

All illustrations are original color artwork/photos converted to grayscale renderings, courtesy of Anthony Abbate.

Resource Publications
An imprint of Wipf and Stock Publishers
199 W. 8th Ave., Suite 3
Eugene, OR 97401

www.wipfandstock.com

ISBN 13: 978-1-62564-220-2

Manufactured in the U.S.A.

This book is dedicated to my teachers in the Loyola Institute for Ministry Program at Loyola University, New Orleans, who taught me how to see God in the world and to interpret that presence as grace.

Contents

List of Illustrations / ix
Preface / xi
Introduction to Advent: How to Use This Book / xiii
Prologue: Overview of the Advent Season / xv

Day 1 *Cosmic Christ* / 1
Day 2 *Life* / 2
Day 3 *The Beach* / 3
Day 4 *Dawn* / 4
Day 5 *Presence* / 5
Day 6 *Church* / 6
Day 7 *Overnight* / 7
Day 8 *Yielding* / 8
Day 9 *Morning* / 9
Day 10 *Paradox* / 11
Day 11 *Newborn Life* / 12
Day 12 *Company* / 13
Day 13 *Celestial Dreams* / 14
Day 14 *The Nature of Light* / 15
Day 15 *Sickness* / 16
Day 16 *Vision* / 18
Day 17 *Pregnancy* / 19
Day 18 *Preparation* / 20

Day 19 *Hurry* / 21
Day 20 *Gaudate* / 22
Day 21 *Light* / 23
Day 22 *Promise* / 24
Day 23 *Penance* / 25
Day 24 *Baby* / 26
Day 25 *Christmas Vigil* / 28
      Incarnation / 30

Epilogue: Canticle of the Season *Desert Rhapsody* / 33

Illustrations

FIGURE 1   Encounter / 1
FIGURE 2   Agave Light / 5
FIGURE 3   Hawk's Perch / 8
FIGURE 4   Ready for Winter / 10
FIGURE 5   Prickly Pear / 13
FIGURE 6   Agave Flower / 14
FIGURE 7   Waiting / 31
FIGURE 8   Winter Blossom / 34

Preface

I LOVE ADVENT—THE COLORS, the feeling, the promise, and yes, it has it stresses. The weather changes, Christmas looms ahead, and there is so much to do to get ready for the holiday. Gifts, cards, cooking, cleaning, travel—events that should be joyful can have their downside. As I immerse myself in the beginning of the church year, a time of new beginnings, I know that what is important is the health of my spirit and my orientation to Advent. Once I recapture that feeling, things fall into place and I realize that the Incarnation in life is messy but paradoxically already pregnant with post-resurrected joy. So too, we all can come to know God through our own experience in the here-and-now of Advent.

Our spirituality is not some abstract concept of heaven, but rather the gospel message of the season empowers us to trust in the mystery of our human nature. By modeling ourselves on the fullest of human beings—Jesus Christ, God's self-gift of mystery from the beginning of time, who entered into the human experience—Advent assumes personal significance. In each historical time and place we can come to know and enter into relationship with God. How could it be otherwise, for God knew each of us before we were in our mother's womb!

The invitation to share in God's life is what we call grace, a gift initiated by God. Grace creates a two-way street where we are not hopelessly constrained by sin but can dynamically respond to God's self in a hopeful and joyful way. This is the spirit by which we should minister, live, and love as the ultimate purpose of life. Humanity and creation, incarnated holy and mysterious places of encounter, comprise integral matrices of our experience as humans.

Preface

Grace acts both as a lens and a compass to help us see our lives more clearly and to understand where we are going. In a world fraught with sin—oppression, poverty, injustice, hunger, illiteracy, illness, or stress—we can still see it as laced with grace. We can stumble in the dark, embrace illness, death, suffering, and disappointment and know God dwells there. Sometimes God is disguised; sometimes God is clear. But, looking to the edge of the horizon, we can call everything we see the face of grace. We can imagine grace for we have seen the love of the Incarnation!

Introduction to Advent

How to Use This Book

ADVENT IS THAT SPECIAL time of preparation that precedes Christmas and marks the beginning of the liturgical year. As the Western calendar comes to an end, the church year begins and we wait in hope for the Lord. Liturgically Advent consists of the four Sundays and the time in between that lead up to the great feast of Christmas, the nativity of Jesus. Advent is a special window that allows grace, like a light, to penetrate our lives. This grace is a friendship that is established between God and us as we more poignantly focus on the meaning of the birth of Christ. It is important to realize that Jesus is already here. He came in time historically, comes to us every Christmas, and can be found incarnated in every moment, in every star, cold wind, or daily challenge.

In this season you too have your own experiences of God. After reading my simple reflection, take a minute and think of how God came to you today—in the smile of a child, the blind eyes of an old man, or the quizzical glance of a young bird. Whether in the anonymity of a busy city or the dearthness of the desert, the invitation beckons—encounter God! Then write down your thoughts, phrases, and images below my poem. They don't have to make a formal poem, for poetry is your experience encapsulated in words. Do a drawing; write down a musical note or a memory.

On the first day of the liturgical year—purple cloaks of comfort and light, hope and regal coming in winter clouds—Advent has arrived again. The sky has changed like the lining of an oyster shell, pearly grey-blue-white. Clouds of apocalyptic horses romp over the

Introduction to Advent

mountains. Rain cleanses the air and washes the trees and the grass before the blanket of snow comes tonight. Today ushers in a joyful day of new beginnings for relationships and the way we look at the world.

The feeling of Advent is one of pregnancy—holding in front of oneself the anticipated joy of new life. A tired beauty rests for a few weeks to be born into the light of his face, the firstborn of creation, the curved touch of his grace on the wings of his Spirit in the spatiality and sacramentality of the cosmos. Let us begin the journey of Advent that is the beginning of our journey of faith by contemplating and responding to the Incarnation in everyday life in word and then translate these words into action and live them.

> *Creator of all things, not constrained by form, your sacred story, your cosmic immortal wholeness dwells forever in your divine imagination. We bend our knee, adoring, to the curvature of divine cosmic love.*

Note: The number of days in Advent varies according to the liturgical calendar. The first Sunday in Advent follows the last Sunday of Ordinary Time, the Feast of Christ the King. In 2013 the first Sunday of Advent happens to be December 1. The poems fit this year's pattern. The poem for Christmas Day is augmented with another for the Christmas Vigil. When the liturgical year differs you can adjust your reading accordingly.

Prologue
Overview of the Advent Season

Advent came in on a purple cloud
a dark horse
with rain in his mane
Winds howling
the dryness is gone
He is coming
it has been explained

Day 1

Cosmic Christ

Dogs' tracks
child's toes
dolphin nose
Golden sands
hold brown coconut water

Driftwood like a stingray's tail
regal palms of earth's split veil
cast-off shrouds
clouds of crowds
parallel the sweet wild beach

Soft jade seas
winds that breathe
world to be
Advent's first day he gives to me

Figure 1: Encounter

Day 2

Life

You visit in sunrise and sickness
wild winds
cool water
Why do I feel the sickness more?
You smile from the dark face of the moon
I swim in a calm lagoon of prayer
Awaiting your answer

While dolphins' bellies smile in praise
Theirs is a day caressed in water
Mine in graspless air
I swoon from your presence
Hot sun blesses my forehead
I can only wait for you
In the deafening calm of Advent

Day 3

The Beach

Ancient new waves
on liquid knees
Diamonds singing holy
at the foot of the shore
Panda skies
flowered dreams
in the place of sand and volcanoes
Iceberg clouds
above tall trees
Honeybees stop to look at me!

Day 4

Dawn

A kiss of pure mist meets morning
Unseen birds breathe aloha
Streetlights and Christmas trees
Kept guard throughout the night
Highways
a rhythmed ribbon of life
renew our daily connection

Day 5

Presence

The moisture of island
is memory
but even in my desert home
I feel you
in winter sun
white light
absence of heat
curious wild life
my goldfishes' delight

Figure 2: Agave Light

Day 6

Church

The regal purple
of the altar
reminds us
you are king
The royal blue
of banners
bears your name for all to see
O Come Emmanuel we pray
Prepare ye
the Baptist says
What do we yearn for?
The empty crèche
awaits
Our hearts
newborn
on Christmas day

Day 7

Overnight

Snow descended overnight
the world looks clean
anointed bright
In case we did not see you then
the tracks of tiny birds therein
mark gentle lives of holy grace
given to us to see your trace

Day 8

Yielding

I leave for Mass
An owl rests in a tree
at the intersection of a yield sign

Crows gathered at a stoplight
take off as we approach
Speed not to exceed 35 mph

Hawks pause
As the Advent sky of opal shells
briefly opens to display
Tahitian pearls in tones of day

An even briefer glimpse
of the paradise they hold
shines coral rose
blushes
at the attention of the setting sun

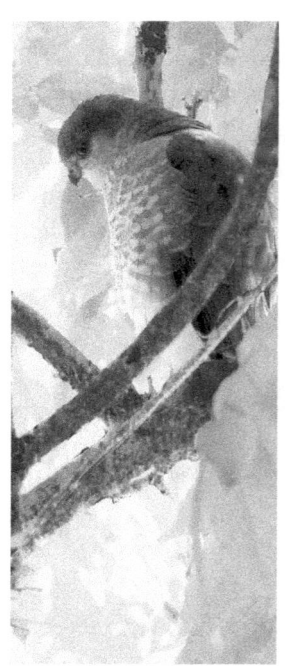

Figure 3: Hawk's Perch

Day 9

Morning

The falling snow alerts them
"Eat. It is cold and you need energy"
They gather by the feeder
in their frenzy
with halting beaks
take time to say
"Thank you for not forgetting us this day"

They line up
one by one
the swinging station
holy communion rail of believers
Others scramble on the ground
to thresh through fallen seeds
Some take time to spar

I stay behind my kitchen window
"Don't worry, there is enough for all
and even when it runs out
I will fill the feeders"
But in their wildness
They clamor in worry
"There will not be enough"
I understand their actions

I watch from the window
steaming hot coffee breathes
"Trust in the one who cares"
They turn back to me and smile

Figure 4: Ready for Winter

Day 10

Paradox

What is there in darkness we need to see?
When we find it
what do we do with it?
It is not our own life
or borrowed gift
Can we bring it to the darkness
and find light again?

Day 11

Newborn Life

The snow reveals
red blue orange white birds' breasts
It falls from roofs
Ice crystals
frozen glitter
soft silk wrappings
small white lights
born from an evergreen
Christmas bells of fancy and delight

Day 12

Company

They gather 'round the simple table
seeds and water
bread and wine
Sun looms low
cold for babies
Time to turn to rocks and vines
Silver thorns peek though snow
Large strange footprints
Precede mine

Figure 5: Prickly Pear

Day 13

Celestial Dreams

Marian blue
mantle sky
Moon a womb
holding your child
A girl so young
God on her mind
She knew the promises
to become the mother of them
What could she think
but only hold Him
the angel said

Figure 6: Agave Flower

Day 14

The Nature of Light

The glazed sun reaches
to kiss the curved cheek of earth
She rushes in brushes and fading sky
Snow remains behind
to cover earth in his blanket of white
until the clear sun gets up again
to make his way towards her rose'd face

Day 15

Sickness

Sickness claims no season
to belong only to it
It takes us
in the feverish heat of summer
the cold of December
dry autumn leaves
bewailing spring winds
It wants all of us
in its weighty sinful lust
What can we do when it claims us
takes over our lives
our consciousness
our breath
voice
strength?
Smile
soul
surrender

The ant staggers across the tile
crossing a mile
alone confused
I watch in sadness
Nothing I do

I can only peek
at a small piece of life
Hungry and weak

I walk away
The pace of the day
Hymn hum

Day 16

Vision

The sound of Israel
is in my groaning lungs
They did not know God
be God
when they saw Him
New Israel saw Him a little clearer
Still need to see Him
be Him
He has always been with us
We need to be Him

Day 17

Pregnancy

Mary overshadowed
O come holy one
Israel's old temple
come undone
Mary carries the fulfillment
the promised one
The church is blessed Mary
Thy kingdom come

Day 18

Preparation

Snow dusts the desert
Rock peeks out to look at its cover
Clouds parade through the expanse
Shadowing snow
New blanket of cold
love for the child who will arrive

Day 19

Hurry

The birds can't eat fast enough
The squirrel fills his cheeks
with seeds and nuts and runs away
The snow can't come down fast enough

The people can't buy enough
What are we hungry for?
What do we sense
in the agonizing cold of December?
Hurry the LORD is here!

Day 20

Gaudete

Perfectly decorated
house of light
cards sent
presents wrapped
resistance melted
It is God's time
Time of faith and hope
returns as a season

The Spirit
new blades of grass
take shape beneath frozen snow
in light and darkness
it grows
full of color and resiliency
Spring's promise has arrived
God's love nests
In hide and seek

Day 21

Light

Mysterious papaya
water-colored sky
Grace funneled through the rounded fruit of the womb
On the face of a babe
What is it about water that draws us near to it?
Is it that it can capture light but not contain it?
that we mix in it but do not merge?
that it is fluid freezes falls?
Fish live in it and it is fun
That it is white blue green
We drink it
wash with it
travel to it
It enters and leaves our body
unsame sameness liquid breath

Day 22

Promise

Morning horizon of blue pearls
resting in patches of waiting snow
Sun still hiding
people in bed
old days continuing
new beginnings ahead
Anticipating unfolding
moment of stillness
aloneness
possibility frozen

Strong and squirmy
dead and wormy
mavericked havoc
on the road
Some remember
blackened embers
ground to dust
and winds that sow

Day 23

Penance

He said be grounded
Be peaceful
It is good to be here with you O LORD
I said reconcile
Be peaceful
It is good to be here with you O God

Day 24

Baby

The baby lies so still
eyes wide with wonder
dependent
so easy to love him
just to behold
forever
would be perfection

Soft brown ground
from snow mounds melt
shadows longer than my height
happy birds through earmuffs sing
moon in blue skies
sun in rings
winter's sleeping
stirs for spring

Oh child of nature
Announced on a cloud
Your mind a spotless shroud
Oh embryo of youth
Blooming like a flower
Sweet as an April shower
If your mind can comprehend

The humanity of men
You still want to know
You still want to sow
your earth

Day 25

Christmas Vigil

Christmas night
holy lights
Few cars on the highway
driving to destinations
of anticipation

Midnight will pass
A marriage human and divine
Wills comprising hope
treasured gift of love
no other gift can match

We keep waiting hoping celebrating
rain falling
cool union of heaven and earth
purple fog
humility
connection
the prompting of unsatisfied religion
dreams of transcendental merging
wild blue wave of communion

Sunrises sunsets
promise and fulfillment

eternal agelessness
anticipation
untamed horse of nature and destiny

O wondrous galaxy of grace
cradle of the human race
Heaven's throne
Awaits your face

Incarnation

Finding God in thickets
is like finding him in crickets
no beginning ending middle
only constant drones of love
Amen alleluia
I am in you
I can hear you
I have made you
I have loved you
from the stars that are my home

There's a deliciousness to Christmas
Like a Sunday afternoon
Tired after longing
Sadness gladness
A young mother's empty womb

New life
peaceful rabbits
graze outside my little room
Seeking sweetness and a deep sleep
as the daylight turns to moon

The womb the tomb
The same grey place
Where quickened emptied life meets grace
and love takes on the human face

That's the emptiness to Christmas
Unwrapped present is the tomb!

Figure 7: Waiting

Epilogue: Canticle of the Season

Desert Rhapsody

Russian thistle
Sacred missal
God of glory greenness light
O love divine

Lizards napping
Sparrows clapping
Bunnies hopping honeyed flight
O love they chime

Cacti glowing
Coyotes crowing
Come and prance its grace tonight
O love be mine

Fluid glory
Unhurried story
Nothing is too big or slight
O love be mine

Teach your children
Stubborn
willing
All is love within your sight

O love divine

FIGURE 8: Winter Blossom

www.ingramcontent.com/pod-product-compliance
Lightning Source LLC
Chambersburg PA
CBHW061516040426
42450CB00008B/1641